To See Clearly
A Portrait of David Hockney

Abrams Books for Young Readers
New York

Just as the sun peeked through the windows,
young David Hockney rubbed the sleep from his eyes
and put on his glasses.

He tiptoed downstairs to collect the daily newspaper and studiously began to fill any empty space on the paper with drawings. In England during World War II, paper was hard to come by, so David had to use what he could find. He drew on top of his dad's comics. He drew on his mother's family chore list. When he ran out of space, he even drew on the linoleum floors. His mother finally said *Enough!* and got David a blackboard so he wouldn't end up drawing on the wallpaper!

David never had enough space. There were seven of them in the cramped house in Bradford, Yorkshire. The air was full of soot from wool mills that blackened the old stone buildings and the skies. But the Hockney household was full of books, art, and love.

David and his siblings would often spend time in a nearby grove of trees, observing the insects and birds as they went about their days. David liked how drawing made him look more carefully at things. He found that when he sat down to draw one blade of grass, suddenly he started to see all the other blades of grass around it.
The more he looked and drew, the more he saw.

On weekends, David loved going to the cinema with his father. There he could travel beyond the cramped, smoggy streets of Bradford to the sunlit streets of Hollywood, even if just for a few hours. He loved how the movies opened new worlds to him. Could skies anywhere really be as bright, clear, and sunny as they seemed in California? For those few hours, time seemed to slow down.

David was good at school—so good that he was accepted into the prestigious Bradford Grammar School. But when he learned that he would no longer be taught art there, David decided to take matters into his own hands: He would spend all his time drawing anyway! He drew all over his assignments—he didn't care about his grades, or even if they expelled him.

His mother, seeing him struggle, stepped in and found an art teacher who agreed to give David private lessons for free. David's grades improved, and he could see more clearly what he wanted to learn.

With his school life back on track, David started
to see himself more clearly, too. He had his first
crush, on another boy named David, while on a
Boy Scouts camping trip. David didn't know what
this meant for him, but he knew it was exciting.

At sixteen, all his drawing paid off, and he was accepted at the Bradford School of Art. Finally, school was a place where he could learn the types of things *he* wanted.

In school, David worked harder than ever, determined not to waste any time. But when the teachers critiqued his work, David learned that they were seeing a lot more than he was. "I hadn't looked hard enough," he realized, and so he resolved to work even harder.

To be somewhere that challenged him was a thrill!

And no one complained when he drew all over his assignments.

During art school, David saved up enough money to go with his class to London for the first time, to visit the museums and galleries that the big city had to offer. When he went to an exhibition of Pablo Picasso's work, David felt his mind open up. Some people didn't like Picasso; they said he didn't really know how to draw. But David knew better.

Picasso used drawing and painting
to rearrange the world the way
he wanted to. David liked the way
Picasso tried to see things from
all different sides at once.

After David visited the big city, he was hooked! So when it came time for him to go to college, he chose the Royal College of Arts in London. There, David started to make friends with fellow artists, including Adrian, the first openly gay person David had ever met. Being gay was illegal in England in the 1950s, and David felt such joy to find a friend who lived without hiding. He began to put those feelings of freedom into his paintings. He worked tirelessly, and gallery owners began to take notice of his work.

But although he was finding his voice as an artist, David still felt stifled by the gray skies of England. One night, after seeing a Lady Clairol hair color commercial on television, David convinced his friends to add a little more sunshine to their lives. "Blondes have more fun," he declared. It was time for a change! After David graduated from school, he saved his money to finally turn this childhood dream into reality. David was going to Hollywood.

As he stepped off the plane, the sun
seemed so much brighter, the air sweeter
and cleaner, and the spaces and the ocean
felt infinite. Palm trees! Surfers! Swimming
pools! Everything seemed to pulse with
color and excitement.

David especially loved looking at the swimming pools. He enjoyed the way you could see the surface of the water, but also see through it to what was underneath. He felt that there was always more than one way to see something—and that the more carefully you looked, the more possibilities opened up.

He also liked the way painting made time slow down. He once spent two weeks depicting a giant splash of water that had only existed for a couple of seconds in real life!

David loved making portraits of
his friends, too—all that time
spent sitting with them and
looking at them carefully. He
felt that the better he knew a
person, and the more clearly
he saw them, the more
their personality showed
up in his art.

Just like with water, he looked through the surface and painted what was underneath.

One summer, David fell in love. He and Peter were inseparable, and David couldn't stop drawing and painting him. Even though Los Angeles was more accepting than England at the time, it was still very daring for David to put scenes of gay life into his paintings. He was one of the first painters to do it, and it shocked people. But David didn't mind. "They want to be ordinary," he said. "They want to fit in. Well, I don't care about that. I don't care about fitting in."

David's paintings of California started gaining him worldwide attention, and before long he was on his way to fame. His first exhibition in the United States sold out. Wealthy art collectors, museums, and galleries wanted more and more of his work. But even more exciting—regular people did, too. His show at the Los Angeles County Museum of Art attracted more visitors than any other contemporary artist they'd shown!

People were falling in love with the way he looked at the world and the beauty he saw in it.

David tried to find beauty during difficult times, too. He lost many friends as he grew older, particularly during the AIDS crisis in the 1980s and '90s. When his friends were sick, he would make paintings for them, of flowers that would never stop blooming. When a close friend back home in Yorkshire became sick with cancer, David decided it was time to return to England. He began to paint the rolling Yorkshire hills and brought the canvases to the hospital to cheer his friend up.

Now when David saw the landscapes of his old country, all the good memories of his childhood filled his eyes. "As we get older," he thought, "memory becomes more meaningful. We might forget things, but you've got to forget to remember anyway." After all the time that had passed, he was able to look more carefully and see how beautiful England really was.

He painted the landscapes around his home every day, seeing them with new eyes. He drove the countryside, painting outdoors with bright colors and bold patterns. He watched the seasons change, slowing them down with each painting he made.

And he always kept searching for new ways to see. He made art with computers, cameras, and fax machines, and at seventy began painting on his iPhone. He studied the *camera obscura*, which used mirrors to help Renaissance painters to draw.

He had exhibitions of paintings he made
on iPads, and he even took pictures with
nine different video cameras at once
to try and see the world from different
perspectives at the same time.

He never got bored of finding new perspectives. And the world didn't get tired of it either! Even after he'd become a famous painter, he was never content to do the same thing he'd done before. He made enormous paintings across dozens of canvases, designed opera productions, and became one of the most popular painters in the world, bringing joy to millions with his work. He had come a long way from his little house in Bradford, and now, no one minded if he wanted to paint on their walls (or swimming pools)!

But as he got older, there was never enough time.
At seventy-five, he was so busy, he didn't even have
time to paint the queen of England when she asked!
(He did design a stained-glass window for her cathedral
in Westminster Abbey, though.) There was never enough
time to spend with friends, to paint, to look, or to learn.
But David knew a secret.

He knew that the only way to slow time down was to stop and look more carefully. And that the more time you take to look, the more you see how beautiful life can be.

"I think I am seeing more clearly now than ever."
—David Hockney, age seventy-four

"It's the very process of looking at something that makes it beautiful."
—David Hockney

David Hockney was born on July 9, 1937, in Bradford, a small city in the Yorkshire region of England. After graduating from the Royal College of Art in London and moving to Los Angeles in the 1960s, he quickly rose to fame with his paintings of swimming pools, gay life, and midcentury LA. His immense career spans over sixty years, and throughout it he has excelled at drawing, painting, printmaking, photography, and stage design. He is one of the most influential British artists of the twentieth century and one of the most popular and beloved living artists. In 2020, at the age of eighty-three, he moved to Normandy, France, where he lives and paints with his longtime companion and assistant, Jean-Pierre Gonçalves de Lima.

AUTHOR'S NOTE

I remember walking through the David Hockney retrospective at the Metropolitan Museum of Art in New York in 2017 and feeling the enormous weight and excitement that comes with seeing an artist's life's work laid out in front of you. It is the feeling of being given the gift of seeing what is possible, and knowing you'd better get to work. The subtitle here is *A Portrait of David Hockney*, because I knew there would be no way to cover his entire life in one book, so I thought of this project as if I were painting a single portrait of him, and about what I wanted to show. His work is skilled, inventive, varied, and full of joy. As a gay artist myself, it was especially powerful to see his fearlessness, and all that he was able to accomplish beginning in a time and place in which it was illegal to be gay. But beyond that, what inspires me most about David Hockney's work is his relentless curiosity and love of life. The ability to get up every day and choose to see more beauty in the world is one of the greatest gifts an artist can give.

"Drawing makes you see things clearer, and clearer, and clearer still."
—David Hockney

HOCKNEY QUOTATIONS CITED

"I hadn't looked hard enough": From Christopher Simon Sykes, *David Hockney: The Biography—1937–1975, A Rake's Progress.* New York: Nan A. Talese, 2012.

"Blondes have more fun": From Christopher Simon Sykes, *David Hockney.* For Lady Clairol campaign, 1956–early 1960s, see en.wikipedia.org/wiki/Clairol.

"They want to be ordinary": From Simon Hattenstone, "David Hockney: 'Just because I'm cheeky, doesn't mean I'm not serious.'" *Guardian*, May 9, 2015. See www.theguardian.com/ artanddesign/2015/may/09/david-hockney-interview-cheeky-serious.

"As we get older, memory becomes more meaningful": From "Picasso: Paintings of the 1960s, introduction by Mimi Poser—David Hockney." Solomon R. Guggenheim Museum Archives, Reel-to-Reel collection (A0004). April 3, 1984.

"I think I am seeing more clearly now than ever": From "David Hockney (artist interview)." *Harper's Bazaar*, November 20, 2011. See www.harpersbazaar.com/culture/art-books-music/a839/david-hockney-interview-1211.

"It's the very process of looking at something that makes it beautiful": From Jonathan Griffin, "Not Interested in That Sort of Thing." *Brooklyn Rail*, October 2014. See brooklynrail.org/2014/10/ criticspage/not-interested-in-that-sort-of-thing.

"Drawing makes you see things clearer": See www.thedavidhockneyfoundation.org/chronology/2020.

"The source of art is love": From Will Gompertz, "David Hockney Shares Exclusive Art from Normandy, as 'a Respite from the News." BBC, April 1, 2020. See www.bbc.com/news/entertainment-arts-52109901.

"The source of art is love."
—David Hockney

HOCKNEY ARTWORKS REFERENCED

We Two Boys Together Clinging, 1961

Beautiful and White Flowers, 1966

A Bigger Splash, 1967

Christopher Isherwood and Don Bachardy, 1968

Mr and Mrs Clark and Percy, 1970–71

Sur la Terrasse, 1971

Portrait of an Artist (Pool with Two Figures), 1972

My Parents, 1977

Peter Schlesinger with Scarf, 1977

Swimming Pool with Reflection (Paper Pool 5), 1978

Mulholland Drive: The Road to the Studio, 1980

Celia II, 1984

A Walk around the Hotel Courtyard, Acatlán, 1985

Photography is dead, Long live painting, 1995

The Road Across the Wolds, 1997

The Arrival of Spring in Woldgate, East Yorkshire in 2011 (twenty eleven), 2011

The Queen's Window at Westminster Abbey, 2018

To my husband, Chris, for helping me slow down
and see how beautiful life can be

The illustrations for this book were made with colored pencil, gouache, and crayon.

Cataloging-in-Publication Data has been applied for and may be obtained from the Library of Congress.

ISBN 978-1-4197-5290-2

Text and illustrations © 2023 Evan Turk
Book design by Pamela Notarantonio

Printed and bound in China
10 9 8 7 6 5 4 3 2 1

Abrams Books for Young Readers are available at special discounts when purchased in quantity for premiums and promotions as well as fundraising or educational use. Special editions can also be created to specification. For details, contact specialsales@abramsbooks.com or the address below.

Abrams® is a registered trademark of Harry N. Abrams, Inc.

ABRAMS The Art of Books
195 Broadway, New York, NY 10007
abramsbooks.com